Scientific Writing

From

Scratch

Scientific Writing From Scratch: How to write Your first Research Paper

Radhika Vijay

Dedicated

To

"Lord Krishna"

Copyright © 2022 Radhika Vijay

Foreword

This book is very near and dear to me as when I started to
write a research article, it was a great struggle for me,
I am still learning and there is no end to perfection.
But the thing I learnt is-
"It is better to be done than perfect."
And so do I advise you all the same.
Do not delay your first research article, there is no point in it.
It will never be perfect, so complete it and
Experience the joy of having a published article
Of your own in your hands!!
Being a student of science or medicine or any subject
involving research, you deserve this and should go for it.
For all the guidance and details of steps
in order to publish your first article, I have
Covered almost all essential points and aspects that you
Need to follow, enact and exercise.
Hope this piece of Scientific literature serves your purpose
And make your dreams come true!
All the best!!

Don't forget to subscribe to my free
E-Newsletter by simply signing up at
https://www.ispharmacologydifficult.com
. It contains a lot of updates about
drugs, medicines, health and my
podcast updates also. And now the
Author updates section will be added
to let you all know more!

Table Of Contents

CHAPTER 1

INTRODUCTION

During medical graduation, there is no burden of research and publishing articles. Students are hardly concerned about these terms, journals etc. Books are the centre of study these days.

But once you enter post graduation or higher studies in any field, you suddenly realise the term "research" is being used quite often.

As a new admission, as far as my experience says, the grapes are quite sour and it doesn't seem like one's cup of tea! Right? Well, these were my ideas as a newbie student while pursuing post graduation.

But the motto of this work of literature is not bound by any particular course or subject. Neither am I an expert of research or publishing many articles. I have too tried and strived for my articles and publications in a very similar manner as an average student does and I have experienced the hardships of a new researcher in the same way as everyone does!

—

Every research is done according to a *Protocol* plan which are nothing but guidelines to conduct any successful research.(2)

Its main components include-IMRAD

- INTRODUCTION-Title of study, Research topic and background and Objectives of study
- METHODS-Materials and methods includes study design, sample size, data collection and data analysis
- RESULTS- of the study
- AND
- DISCUSSION-includes discussion, strengths and limitations of a study and Conclusion

And yes, I am still all the time facing new unidentified issues and difficulties whenever I plan to undertake a new research project, actually that's the whole process and none of the steps given in this book can be skipped. So accept the new challenges and hurdles while doing any new research because that's the way it is!

My aim in writing this book is simply to make the students, especially fresh and new learners aware of the very basics of writing a research article. While they will learn the basics, slowly and steadily they will be going through the unskippable steps to write their first research article.

Yes, you got it right. My promise is for the first article for sure and like "Save the Cat" (by Blake Snyder) works for every story writer as a wonderful tool to draft and plot their stories, novels etc, the basic steps in this book can be used again in case you feel like publishing more articles or follow a similar pattern.

Nowadays it is not only the need but also the responsibility of highly expert and skilled clinicians who practise *evidence based medicine*, to answer relevant, important and valuable research questions in the form of proper study and also make everyone aware of the end results and findings of the research.

I aim to cover the steps to publish quite basic, simple quality articles which can be accepted in some good journals. The quality and upto an extent the authenticity of the article is all that matters! There are many different types of studies, researches and articles. The study ranges from basic to highly complicated multicenter trials.

But again, I want to make this clear that this book will make you publish your first article, later it's obvious and expected that as you grow in your field and your career, your knowledge about research will grow manifold and so will your experience and your contacts. And when these all will add up, your research area and quality will too nurture!

And additionally, I want to make clear that the whole book is about writing only—-----"__ORIGINAL RESEARCH ARTICLE__"

__NOT__

Reviews/Meta Analysis/ Short Communications/ Opinions/Clinical Trials/Case reports/meeting Reports/Letters to Editor/ New Drug Updates/Commentaries/Correspondences, etc.

For the time being, without any delay let us know the steps to write your first research article….

CHAPTER 2

STEP 1-RESEARCH IDEA

First and foremost, when you sit down to write with your pen and paper, you actually do not know what to write, where to start?

Now the reason is that your brain is lacking ideas. You need to fill your brain with some ideas. Now, how to go about this thing?

Before you grab your notebook to scribble anything, you have to get ideas for your research.

"Prior and Proper planning prevents poor performance"

A good research question can significantly add to the research pool of the chosen topic and help colleagues and co-researchers by providing valuable insights and inferences while poor research question will not only spoil your first impression as a researcher, will turn down your influence, expose your weaknesses and create hurdles and resistance in conductance of smooth research.(1)

A "FINER" Criteria as stated by Hully etal may serve a decent guide while choosing a perfect research idea. It stands for - **F**easible, **I**nteresting, **N**ovel, **E**thical and **R**elevant research idea!(1)

Sources of research ideas:

1. Journals from library
2. Journals on internet
3. Articles on internet

4. Your own research field of interest
5. Your own research idea of choice

To begin with, you need to find the reputed journals of your subject from the library or on the internet and without any effort, have a look at the current issue and start reading from the top end.

Second approach is to find certain articles or article titles on the internet, even if you type related terms, you will get many articles from different journals and you can start reading them.

Thirdly is the approach when there is a dormant idea, some midway thought, some incomplete word in your mind which makes no sense but the best part is that you can google it by writing the half or incomplete sentence or term or your made up sentence and write the term "research article" or simply "article" as suffix and press enter.

And lo! You will be amazed to find a lot many articles of your self-woven terms or sentences which actually prevail in different journals. The best thing is that you realise that you have found something related to your choice or wish.

I think the best situation is the third one but still if you are a blank blackboard, let google write something on it with its chalk.

This whole tedious exercise will help you reach one most important *Research Question* of your study!

So, this is the first step, you have "food for thought", you have kindled an idea , that is great news!

CHAPTER 3

STEP 2-START RESEARCH FROM SCRATCH

Now you have to collect all the studies of your interest at one place. Different methods can be tried:

1. Save as pdf files or downloads
2. Copy and paste text in one MS Word document
3. Get hard copy of the articles collected

Do whatever suits you best, there is no defined method here, anyone can be followed.

Once you have collected the desired articles, it is now time to go through each one of them. Yes, you need to invest time and attention to read these articles. This will help to fill your brain with much required terms, ideas and strategy of your own to proceed further.

This is actually a time consuming step, but the time invested will pay you in future when you are actually writing the article.

What to do while you read the article:

1. Pay special attention to the title- this will be a guiding step for you to articulate or craft the title of your research paper.
2. Always highlight the relevant and important lines, information, terms and definitions that can guide you in while crafting your own article
3. As you proceed, you are in fact figuring out the present and absent information or better known as *knowledge gap*

4. Cross out the undesirable paragraphs or lines which you will never turn back to or which hold no value related to your article

5. Additional higher level steps which can help you improve upon this process of *Review of Literature* is:
    - Consulting experts in the field of interest
    - Interviewing focus groups/patients
    - Conducting *systematic reviews*
    - Conducting *pilot studies*
    - Conducting *exploratory analysis*

This way you have actually summarised the articles also and the second reading will be quite selective, to the point and time saving.

TOPIC OF THE STUDY:

First you decide the context of your study broadly, i.e. what it will all about, this will guide the Title of the study.

TITLE OF THE STUDY:

A good title should:

- Be consisting of required limited/few words
- Convey the main idea of the study
- Convey the purpose of research question
- Include study design/type or describing words for the study in short.
- (Can) Include study place

ABSTRACT :

Generally every research paper is preceded with an "Abstract".

What is an Abstract?

An Abstract is a short summary of the research paper which you are actually planning to write. It should be well understood that both published and unpublished articles can have an abstract but I will be telling you about unpublished article's Abstract first. Since you are on your way to write an article, you have incomplete information to furnish in an Abstract.

Generally Abstracts are of 250-300 words and be specific depending upon the Journal you choose. Structure your Abstract in heads like:

- Background/Introduction includes 3-4 sentences about present study research question, gaps it covers and little about past studies done in the context.
- Methods includes study sample(tentative), study design, data collection and analysis tools
- Results include what will be derived most importantly and targeted results in future tense without any data.
- Conclusion includes what is the aim of study as a conclusion finally at present time (I mean before you have written your research article)
- Key Words : Usually 3-5 important key words are more than enough around which the complete study revolves.

CHAPTER 4

STEP 3- COLLECT DATA

Now a rough skeleton of your desired study is in your head, but till it is not formed into something tangible, it makes no sense.

Now once you will feel overflooded with information, thoughts and ideas and there are many rather maximum chances that you have a totally new idea of a study or research.

That is perfectly fine and not to be worried upon, sit back, hold on to everything known and do not run after the unknown.

Now on a notebook paper, make a list of old research ideas and upcoming new research ideas. Now just read them with full concentration. Generally, it happens that old and new ideas are quite similar and shaping them into two different research articles with only slight differences does not make any sense, Right?

But if something totally different, interesting, elaborative and novel strikes you, then never miss a chance to write it down, along with it, write down the reference or source of the idea.

Again a friendly reminder:

DO NOT SKIP ANY STEP

Now decide upon your first idea to be executed in form of research paper, some good points to follow while choosing your idea are:

1. It should be simple, not complicated
2. It should be quickly doable, if you find it at present out of your reach, drop it at once.
3. It should involve minimal expenses
4. It should be executable by maximum 1-2 people including you yourself
5. It should involve simple basic statistics
6. Keep the sample size feasible, not too large.
7.

It should seem like a long clear road in front of you where you can drive readily without delay and difficulty.

When the first topic is chosen, it is the time to ACT!

Yes, now you need to collect the data for your research.

Since you have chosen a simple topic, definitely you have a way or means in your mindset to collect data. Some easy ways are as follows:

1. Questionnaires- digital/hardcopy
2. Simple medicine intervention
3. Surveys by verbal interviews
4. Retrospective data (medical records)
5. Clinical case/examination
6. Laboratory test reports

7. Information of tools and instruments used for collection of data and methods of testing their reliability and validity (2)

Achieve data collection from the desired number of participants. Once you fulfil the sample size, this task is over.

CHAPTER 5

STEP 4-CONSOLIDATE THE DATA

Now I assume you have chosen a simple study involving descriptive statistics. So, without acting lazy, you need to enter the collected data in your excel worksheet. This is known as creating a Master Chart.

Start the columns with demographic details of patients.

One quick tip:

PATIENT NAMES ARE NEVER INVOLVED IN ANY CALCULATION OR INTERPRETATION.

Create proper heads and subheads in the excel sheet. Generally you need to carry a notebook while doing this work.

Assign different variables- different numerals or alphabets or short abbreviations and simultaneously keep on noting down their complete meaning and description in the notebook.

Again a friendly reminder:

DO NOT SKIP ANY STEP

This is a very time consuming task and should be done very accurately with full patience. Rechecking is highly advisable!

You cannot move further without completing this step, so even if bored, do not start anything else, rather take a break, but first finish this task. Hope you understand the essence of this step and also the importance of the stepwise process.

CHAPTER 6

STEP 5- ANALYSE THE DATA

After finishing off with variables and different columns in the master chart, it's the time for "*Analysis*"

You have to deeply and carefully observe the master chart. And do not forget to keep a notebook in your hand for quick calculations and notes.

Generally it is a good approach to analyse demographic details of the patients initially.In these are included heads like age, gender, income, employment, education level, etc. Make your own groups of convenient ranges for age, education and income levels. Keep the ranges wide and not too narrow to make multiple groups that hinder and exhaust the calculation process.

This is an apt time to set your inclusion and exclusion criterias as far as age group is concerned.(Note this in your notebook). Also, calculate average age of the sample size(By calculating mean)

Now when you have finished setting ranges for different groups, analyse and assign the patient count to each group accurately. Keep on reverse checking.

It is a good idea to take help of a statistician at this point, especially if the sample size is too big.

Next step is to analyse other columns of drugs, diseases, treatment, follow up, etc

Each column should be assessed separately for clear, accurate results. Do not mess into many columns at a time. You will surely get a headache then :)

Keep on noting everything in the notebook, do not miss a single point that will serve a reference in future.

CHAPTER 7

STEP 6- START WRITING

Now you have done the lengthy tedious task of assessment and analysis of the master chart thoroughly. It is the time to start writing your real work document.

There are different sections of the research paper like:

1. Background/Introduction
   - Review of Literature
   - Gap
   - Question
2. Materials and Methods
   - Sample size
   - Study design & setting
   - Inclusion & Exclusion criteria
   - Ethical approval
   - Statistics applied
3. Results
4. Discussion
   - Summary
   - Conclusion

Amongst the above listed sections, you can actually write your research article from the beginning or even you can start writing from the end.

You will notice that some of these sections are purely separate and independent of each other and that gives you freedom to initiate your writing from either end!

In the first approach:

Background and Introduction can be easily initiated from the different studies you have collected, from your own experience and observation during data collection and the basic motto and idea of your research question.

It requires to be furnished in the end once all the sections are written completely, you can modify, add or delete the initial statements, some findings, some important statements etc.

In the Second approach:

You can begin your writing from the results section, since you have completed the analysis of your master chart thoroughly with tools of excel sheet, charts, diagrams and pivot tables.

It is actually very simple, just start writing the calculated details right away without any fancy discussion. Keep the pattern the same, maintain the homogeneity all throughout the results- give numbers for all results or ratios or percentages, etc. This adds to the reading joy of the article.

TABLES AND FIGURES:

- Number of tables and figures is in accordance with the journal you are choosing generally.
- It is a good idea to keep the ratio equal for tables and figures
- Not all results require tables and figures.
- Always make the figures in excel sheet using pivot tables, then copy and paste to your word document
- Legend data/heads should be written/displayed in figures.
- Tables should be made in word document
- Tables should be made for lists, comparisons, similar kinds of bulky data and do not mention the table data in text.
- Figures should be made for most important and significant findings of the study and not all the results.
- Choose both types of figures- bar charts (vertical & horizontal) and pie charts to make study look better and expressive.
- Legend data/heads should be displayed in figures too. Choose coloured figures over black and white until and unless specified.
- Avoid 3D figures, not required at all.

CHAPTER 8

STEP 7- MATERIALS & METHODS

Materials and methods section is an independent section and includes details of sample size, study design, study setting, inclusion and exclusion criteria and statement of ethical approval.

Methodology defines the approach to achieve the exact goals and objectives(2)

PICOT approach is very useful in defining various components of the study, it stands for- **P**opulation, **I**ntervention, **C**ohort group, **O**utcome, **T**ime of study(1)

By following this group, Inclusion and Exclusion criteria and assessment methods for the study can be easily undecided upon.(1)

As a beginner, you have to simply decide upon a study sample, focussed and measurable outcome measures and time of study. (1) Interventions can be avoided if non reachable and complicated

What is the right time to write this section?

It is a nice idea to write this section details after completing your data collection.

Parts of Materials & Methods:

- Study design: There can be different types of study designs like cross sectional, cohort, RCT , etc. The type of study should be compulsorily, clearly and completely stated. Proper selection of study design ensures accuracy in results,(2) hence guidance and help from experts like statisticians should be thoroughly sought. For the first research paper, the simplest and easiest study design should be chosen.
- Study population: This includes correct and proper explanation of eligibility criteria, inclusion and exclusion criteria to choose the subjects for the study. It also covers randomization and blinding to minimise bias in study (2)
- Sample size: Under this head, we have to cover important aspects like "Informed consent", Economic constraints and Ethical parameters and approval. Sample size is based on the power of the sample and includes proper sampling technique. All these are mentioned in detail under this head.(2)

NOTE- Ethical considerations should be in accordance with the Declaration of Helsinki i.e. details of risks and benefits should be mentioned. Details of alternative treatments, confidentiality of participants, freedom of withdrawal from study and data safety should be mentioned and conveyed to all the subjects of the study.(2)

You can initially draft an outline as far as sample size is concerned.

Study setting covers the place where study is conducted, it should include specific area of the hospital, department name, name of college and/or the hospital, the city, state and country.

Inclusion and Exclusion criteria though pre-decided becomes more clear once the data collection begins.

Ethical approval statement is mentioned in this section and should include the reference number and date of approval.

Statistics (test or procedure) applied should also be stated. This section includes two important information:

1. Data collection methods and tools in detail like survey/questionnaire/interview etc and its mode (online/offline) and an account of its validity and accuracy.
2. Statistical analysis tools/software/method etc should also be mentioned.

Advice from statisticians should be sought and is highly recommended.

TYPES OF STUDIES:

- Broadly, study designs are of two major types- Observational and Experimental.
- Observational study can be either Descriptive or Analytical
- Experimental studies involve intervention which test association between exposure and outcome. They can be

done with or without comparisons. These generally include different types of trials like RCT.
- Descriptive studies can be case reports, cross sectional study, cohort study or ecologic study.
- Cohort study can be Prospective or Retrospective in nature.

METHODS TO REDUCE BIAS IN A STUDY:

- Randomisation
- Blinding
- Placebo

OVERVIEW OF STATISTICAL TESTS:

When data is normally distributed (means):

- To compare 2 data sets, you can use paired/unpaired t-test.
- To compare more than 2 data sets, different types of ANOVA tests can be used.
- For association and Regression, you can choose correlation and regression tests respectively.

When data is not normally distributed (median):

- For comparison of 2 data sets, you can choose types of Wilcoxon test.
- For comparison of more than 2 data sets, you can use Friedman or Kruskal Wallis test.
- For association and regression, you can choose correlation and regression tests respectively.

When data is given as proportions:

- For comparison of 2 data sets, you can choose, Mc Nemar's or Fisher's test.
- For comparison of more than two data sets, you can choose Cochrane or Chi-square test.
- For association and regression , you can choose coefficient and regression analysis tests respectively.

CHAPTER 9

STEP 8- DISCUSSION & CONCLUSION

This step is essentially written after completing the Results section. Discussion and Conclusion are generally written separately but sometimes may be written sequentially as one heading.

Differences between Discussion and Conclusion-

1. Discussion involves comparison of one's own study with similar other studies.
2. As and when comparison is made, explanation of the differences is also made simultaneously which is also a part of Discussion.
3. Inference after comparison and possible basis or explanation of difference or similarity amongst the available studies is generally written as Conclusion.
4. References are almost every time a part of the Discussion section.
5. Conclusion generally is devoid of references and is a solid summary of inferences, learnings, current and future scope and improvements and important point of view about the study.
6. Most important results may be stated in the conclusion, but should be highly significant findings of the study and should be stated briefly.

How is Discussion of a Study done?

Steps to follow to start writing the discussion of a study:

- Start with a brief account of study importance and basis, a paragraph of 3-4 lines
- Pick up each result one by one
- Have all the other studies opened in hand at the same time
- For every result, match and find similar finding in other studies and in your notebook make two accounts one for similarity , one for differences of the findings while comparing with other studies
- There should be 4 columns while you compare your study with other studies:

Similarity with other study	Difference with other study	Unique finding found in other study, not accounted in your study	Unique finding found in your study, not accounted in other studies
Study name or number	*Study name or number*	*Study name or number*	*Study name or number*
details	details	details	details

- It's a good practice to write down serial wise other studies as you compare each result with them, this will help you create the reference list later on and also you will easily write the correct order of references as and when they occur in the study.
- Possible explanations of the similarity and the differences with other studies should be stated after each comparison
- Unique findings which are present in other studies and not at all covered in one's own study are stated as *"Limitations of the study"*
- Unique findings which are found only in one's own study and not accounted in other studies are stated as *"Strengths of the study"*

How to write Conclusion of the study?

- Most significant results which can be drawn out from the whole study can be stated as one or two sentences in the conclusion, generally without statistical details.
- Negative statements and words are generally avoided in this section of the study.
- Inferences drawn out from the discussion, most relevant are stated in the conclusion section positively.
- Two to three sentences can be written while considering both strengths and limitations of the study while positively stating the facts and room for future improvement and extension of the study.
- Finally a positive, affirmative statement is made which answers the research question of the study or leaves a strong food for thought or curiosity among the readers directly related to the topic of the study.

- All in all Conclusion is written as one (or maximum two) strong paragraph at the end of the study.
- It may be followed by *Acknowledgements* written in two to three sentences
- This is followed by one liner about *Conflicts of interest* and *Sources of funds*

CHAPTER 10

STEP 9- REFERENCES

References are meant to display the source of information you have drawn an idea from or exact matter for comparison or assisting your scientific writing text, etc. It's a means of gratitude and acknowledgement and should be thoroughly and liberally stated in your research paper. In fact, none of the corresponding material should be missed to be cited.

There are many referencing styles but I will be limiting details to one or two only here as rest of the styles are generally not for scientific writing.

The most famous styles in vogue are **Harvard** and **Vancouver** referencing styles.

Features of Harvard Style of Reference:

- It is Author-date style
- Alphabetical listing order is followed especially at the end of the document.
- Get the right source, then start writing-Surnames followed by First and second names Initials, then year, then title of article, then title of Journal preferred in Italics. This is followed by Volume number, issue number and pages in range, whatever known. In case an article has DOI number, it comes in the end.
- Example-

Dixit, MN & Gadwakar, RJ 2008, 'Prescription pattern in Surgery OPD of city in South Orissa', *Journal of Pharmacy,* vol 8, no 3, pg 45-48.

Features of Vancouver style of Reference:

- It is the Author-number style
- Numerical listing order is followed as far as citations are concerned as and when they appear in the research article
- Get the right source, start writing- Surnames of upto 6 authors, initials for their first and second name. After 6 authors, write 'et al', then write the title of the research article, then the title of the Journal. This is followed by the year of publication and then volume and then issue number.Then if you get to know, mention the pages in range and also you can write DOI number.
- Example-

Teller E, Kiwi AJ. Effects of smoking on lungs. Journal of medicine. 2002;4(1):7-10

TIP- Generally Journals provide reference style guides for different types of articles like scientific publications, chapter from book, online citation, book, magazine, etc.

These guides should be thoroughly studied before starting to write your reference list, as there may be slight variations depending upon different journals.

References should be ordered, clear and complete.Every research article or paper need to have references, it means you are considering and acknowledging the studies done on similar topic, field, concern or research question.

It is always a good idea to gather the similar studies of interest and importance and reference them as per need and order in your study (keeping a notebook section for references throughout the study period is actually a very useful habit which prevents hassles while actually listing down the references for your research article). It not only adorns your own study but gives a chance to the reader to identify and read or use any reference from your article as per his/her own discretion.(2)

If you do not acknowledge the borrowed idea from someone else's work or research, the policy is actually defined as *Plagiarism*.The two most common referencing styles adopted generously are the Vancouver style and the Harvard Style of referencing and the former is much in vogue.(2)

ADVICE- Hence for your first research article, follow the Vancouver style of referencing.

Generally the most important Attachment documents with your
research articles are:

- Authorship declaration form: The Names,
  addresses, affiliations of all authors
- Informed consent form
- Approval letter from Ethics Committee
- Questionnaires
- Letter of Conflict of interest

CHAPTER 11

DO's and DON'Ts

List of Do's while writing a research paper/article

- Research question should be answered properly, no misleading, vague or irrelevant data or information should be written.
- Choose the right feasible topic and write the Title correctly.
- Grammar should be correct. Language should be clear and simple.
- Introduction and review of literature should specify the research gap and relevance of the current study being done. Acknowledgements to the studies should not be missed at this time.
- Objectives of the study should be stated clearly and briefly in points.
- All the parts of Materials and Methods should be paid utter heed to. These include sample size, study setting and design, data collection and analysis tools and methods.
- Results should be clear, unambiguous and relevant.
- Discussion should compare as well as explain the results orderly and up to the point. Orderly approach will help in listing references accurately and easily.
- Conclusion should be short, clear and concise.
- Proper referencing should be done in order to acknowledge the contribution of other researchers in your study. None should be missed or stay incomplete.

List of Don'ts while writing a research paper/article

- Do not miss any step of research or writing the article as it may be of great weakness or deficiency in your research paper.
- Take care of the word count as per the journal needs and accordingly shape up the research article. Extra long review of literature should be avoided.
- Do not go off the topic and try to stick to the "Author guidelines" section of the Journal.
- Do not write difficult language and difficult uncommon abbreviations.
- Important information should be included. Significant results should be included while irrelevant data/statistics should be avoided while writing your initial draft of the research article.
- Power of the sample is very important, if less then it should be well explained and justified(2)
- Wrong statistics are to be not written at all, better consult a statistician.
- Results' data should not be repeated in the discussion section again and again, this is important while you stick to the word count.
- Conclusion should not be very long

TIP: To stick to the word count, do not repeat the results in detail in text if you are giving a table or diagram like a chart (bar/pie) for it.

Table data should never be written at all in results nor the details of diagrams are required to be written.

BONUS TIPS TO CHOOSE THE PERFECT JOURNAL FOR PUBLICATION:

- Make a list of known journals in your field, area of research and subject.
- Get the list of Predatory journals in your field, subject and area of research. Absolutely avoid vague and fake journals.
- Find the impact factor and rank of Journal, it may give you good insights when you compare different journals.
- Indexing of the journal is a very good criteria to decide whether you will choose it or not. Nowadays indexing is a must for Web Of Science, NLM, MEDLINE, EMBASE, SCOPUS, etc.
- Scope of the journal is very important as it decides whether your article fits into the Journal or not and you can assess whether it will be accepted or not.
- Try to go for open access journals.(DOAJ journals)

- Peer review process of the journal should be very clearly stated and in complete detail.
- On the journal website, check for grammar or spelling mistakes as that would show the journal quality and standards
- Ethical policy should be clearly stated and generally these are as per ICMJE or COPE guidelines.
- Look for the editor team members and find out if they are quite expert in their field of knowledge, this will mark the quality and standard of the journal.
- Author rights and Copyright policy should be of good standard and should be very clear.
- Publishing time should be paid heed to as for your first research paper, go for less publishing time like 30 days to 45 days, or as per your convenience. Don't go for journals with very long publishing time , it may discourage you and try your patience too!
- Pay attention to Article Publishing charges (APC) of the Journal, they should be affordable and not beyond reach. Do not pay for fast track publications for your first research paper as the charges are quite high.

CHAPTER 12

DIFFERENCES YOU SHOULD KNOW

1. ***Differences between Thesis and Dissertation:***

- Dissertation is lengthier than thesis. Latter is expected to be at least 100 pages and generally students set this target only.
- Dissertation is usually written to attain PhD degree
- Dissertation is expected to be written more skilfully and accurately as compared to thesis which is written to show one's knowledge in expertise in a topic while attaining graduation degree.
- Sample size is generally bigger for a dissertation
- Dissertation is expected to have more o f newer research elements and more of analysis than a thesis.

2. ***Differences between Thesis and Research paper***

- Thesis is written to finally obtain degree in an institution at the end of graduation/post graduation while research article is a part of curriculum while studying for a degree
- Thesis is generally lengthier than a research article.
- Thesis requires supervision while research articles can be written on their own.
- Thesis are a must to obtain a degree while there is no compulsion on research articles unless and until specified.

GLOSSARY

1. **Scientific Writing-** The means by which researchers communicate their work to others using technical skill. It should be relevant, clear and up to the mark. It should be detailed enough so as to communicate the researcher's hard work and point of opinion unambiguously.

2. **Protocol-** A set of properly organised guidelines and methodology so as to conduct a research project without any error or confusion. Steps are stated orderly and tentative descriptions are given to convey the main summary of the research project.

3. **Research Question-** It is the main theme, guiding light of the research project, its answer is given by the research we do. Everything in the research paper should be centred and focussed around a research question.

4. **Knowledge gap-** It is the gap of information between whatever is known from past studies and the intended research question or what isn't covered or updated as compared to past information.

5. **Abstract-** It is a summary of the whole research written before or after publication usually under heads like Background, Methods, Results and Conclusion.

---

6. **Sample size-** It refers to the number of participants who after informed consent and being well informed, participate in the study. It is in fact a part of the population, and not a complete population.

---

7. **Master chart-** It is the chart made in excel sheet in a large tabular manner. It contains the initial raw details and data collected by the researcher. It is the backbone of any study and is worked upon extensively to derive all the results of the study.

---

8. **Analysis-** Analysis involves the main focus of researchers on different elements or components of the study and then using the knowledge to infer something meaningful. It is the initial step of working on data/study elements.

---

9. **Assessment-** It stands for knowing and identifying the standard/level of inferred results after analysis, etc. It does not involve the numerical computation which is more often seen in Evaluation.

---

10. **Evaluation-** It involves tests and working out the gained knowledge from analysis etc to derive relevant conclusions.

---

11. **Study design-** It stands for proper organised methodology/steps done to collect and analyse data of a study.

---

12. **Cross sectional study-** In this type of study, information and data about the participating individuals is collected over a time point or over a time period.

---

13. **Cohort study-** Cohort means a group of individuals, when a researcher follows and measures different factors and outcomes related to this group in a similar fashion, it is called Cohort Study.

---

14. RCT- It stands for Randomised Controlled Trials, it is the gold standard study. As the name states, subjects are randomly assigned to the group to decrease bias in a study.

---

15. Sampling technique- It is the method by which participants are chosen for a sample size. It involves various methods like Cluster sampling, Random sampling, Stratified sampling, etc

---

16. Declaration of helsinki- It was developed by World Medical Association with the motto to conduct a research ethically on human subjects protecting their interests and respect.

---

17. Observational study- In this study, basically the researcher observes the treatment or interventions administered to the patient, he himself does not play that role.

---

18. Experimental study- In this study, the researcher himself administers the treatment or intervention or any method to the participating individuals (in contrast to the observational studies)

---

19. Descriptive study- These studies do not involve analysis, rather simply describe the present happenings in a study sample. They deal with prevalence, incidence, etc.

---

20. Analytical study- These studies involve analysis and defines relations amongst variables/factors. They deal with interventions, exposure, outcome, etc.

---

21. Case reports- These are types of descriptive studies, deal with patient cases, the subject is an individual patient and generally aim to find a new finding in a case, identifying new research questions.

---

22. **Case series-** In this study series, a group of patients are studied who were given similar treatment and then data is observed for all these case report patients.

---

23. **Ecological study-** It is done for the entire population, data is collected for a factor for the whole population and then inference is drawn for the complete population. These are large studies.

---

24. **Prospective study-** In this type of study, the researcher follows the participating individuals in a time period in the future and along with the time passing, fresh information or data is collected.

---

25. **Retrospective study-** In this type of study , the researcher follows the participating individuals in a time period in the past and collects information from already maintained data/records.

---

26. **Bias-** When intentionally an opinion is favoured in a research methodology or an error occurs while interpreting the result with the aim to promote certain results/ point of view over others which is not in fact true

is called Bias. It can occur at any stage of research from beginning to the end. It has many types like information bias, selection bias, etc.

---

27. **Randomisation-** The process of randomly assigning subjects to a group of study in a way everyone gets an equal chance of selection is called randomisation. It ensures minimum bias and accurate results.

---

28. **Blinding-** The process of hiding a study group from other individuals or participants in a study is called blinding. The aim is to reduce bias and it is done in RCTs. Different types are Single blinded, Double blinded, etc

---

29. **Placebo-** Placebo refers to the inactive/dummy chemical preparation used in place of real medicine in a research to the patient. It may help the patient to relieve his few signs and symptoms of the pathology like mental stress, anxiety , etc. Their purpose is to improve results of the study by forming comparison groups.

---

30. **ANOVA-** Analysis of Variance test helps to find out if any modification occurs in dependent variable in accordance to independent variable. It may be of different types like one way, two way, etc.

---

31. **T-test-** This test is done to compare average values or means amongst two study groups. In this, the mean of one group can be compared to the standard value also.

---

32. **Correlation-** It is the test done to identify association between two continuous variables.

---

33. **Regression-** It is the test done to identify relationships between dependent and independent variables. It can be Linear or Logistic regression.

---

34. **Wilcoxon test-** It is a non parametric test to do comparison between two or more paired groups and establish differences amongst them.

---

35. **Mc Nemar test-** It is a non parametric test between paired nominal groups used to find out modifications in proportions for these paired groups.

---

36. **Friedman test-** It is a type of test alternatively used as a non parametric test for repeated measures of one way ANOVA.

---

37. **Fisher exact test-** It is a test to check association between two variables in a non random fashion especially when sample size is less than 20 (n<20)

---

38. **Kruskal Wallis test-** It is a non parametric alternative test for one way ANOVA.

---

39. **Chi square test-** It is a test done for a large sample size to know the difference between observed and expected values. Data is derived from independent random variables/groups.

40. References- The process of listing details about a concept/idea taken from other research articles in full detail at the end of your research article with the aim to acknowledge their contribution in your research paper.

Citations mean only including other's ideas in part of your article while **references** are different as they include all the detailed information like Author's name, Title of research and the Journal, year of publication, volume number, issue number and page numbers, etc.

---

41. Plagiarism- It is the process of borrowing a concept/idea from someone else's research article/ book/etc but not citing it in your research article or not referencing it properly in a way to avoid giving credit to the researcher who's help you have sought.

---

42. Ethics- Proper code of conduct and rules and regulations should be followed while taking care of human subjects, this is called Ethics. There should be respect for subjects, harms should be minimal while benefits should be maximum.

---

43. Conflict of Interest- It refers to any prevalent difference in point of view/ private interest of the authors(>1) conducting the study. In harmony, it is generally stated as "None".

---

44. Informed consent- It is a form made to be filled by the study participants before the study begins and aims to inform them all about the study, its parts, its intervention, methods, risks and benefits and seeks their permission before the study begins.

---

45. Citation- Citing means to deriva an idea or part of someone else's research and modify it to use in your own research article and properly mention them in the references so that readers of your research get to know from where the concept/idea is borrowed.

---

46. Redundant publication- These are duplicate publications in which the author unethically repeats his research work or results in more than one research article and does not provide proper references.

---

47. Salami publication- Intentional process of segregating results of one study in order to publish more than research articles is an unethical procedure known as Salami Publication.

---

48. Predatory journal- These are deceptive, fake journals which exploit and misguide the authors and have a motive to make money in the wrong way by misinterpreting publication policies.

---

49. Study setting- It refers to the physical and social environment in which the study takes place..

---

50. Cochrane database- A library of high standard, independent evidence owned by Cochrane and published by Wiley. It helps in decision making by its vast collection of databases.

REFERENCES

1. Ravindra VM, Kestle JRW. Writing a Clinical Research Question. Neurosurgery. 2019 Jan 1;84(1):12-16. doi: 10.1093/neuros/nyy484. PMID: 30445508.

2. Al-Jundi A, Sakka S. Protocol Writing in Clinical Research. J Clin Diagn Res. 2016 Nov;10(11):ZE10-ZE13. doi: 10.7860/JCDR/2016/21426.8865. Epub 2016 Nov 1. Erratum in: J Clin Diagn Res. 2016 Dec;10 (12):ZZ03. PMID: 28050522; PMCID: PMC5198475.

3. Rout CC, Aldous C. How to write a research protocol.South. African J. Anaesth. Analg.2016 Sep;22(4):101-107

4. Chidambaram AG, Josephson M. Clinical research study designs: The essentials. Pediatr Investig. 2019 Dec 21;3(4):245-252. doi: 10.1002/ped4.12166. PMID: 32851330; PMCID: PMC7331444.

5. Mann CJ. Observational research methods. Research design II: cohort, cross sectional, and case-control studies. Emerg Med J. 2003 Jan;20(1):54-60. doi: 10.1136/emj.20.1.54. PMID: 12533370; PMCID: PMC1726024.

Afterword

Thanks for reading and making up
this far!

Hope the book served your
expectations and purpose!
Wish you all the best for your first Research Paper!!

And you can also subscribe on
different social media like Twitter,
Instagram, Facebook and Youtube.
And once again, don't forget to
subscribe for my E-Newsletter on
www.ispharmacologydifficult.com

Acknowledgements

I especially want to mention a vote of thanks to my family,
especially my son who is always interested in my books and
this serves as a catalyst to my writing ventures!!
Next a great thanks to Mom and
my brother for always being there by my side
through thick and thin!
And never to forget , heartiest thanks to the students,
researchers, future scientists and medical personnel,
"You are the best!"

About The Author

DR RADHIKA VIJAY ,

MBBS, MD Pharmacology

belongs to Bikaner, Rajasthan, India.

She is a faculty in Sardar Patel Medical College, Bikaner.

She has always been an elite student since her school days.

She has been teaching

Medical Pharmacology for the last 10 years now!!

Appreciator of everything brilliant and intelligent in life and.

with an optimistic

attitude and approach she believes

in the value and power of time, prayers and purpose

driven consistency as strong foundation elements in one's life!

You can connect:

Personal Website - https://www.drradhikavijay.com
Podcast Website: https://www.ispharmacologydifficult.com
Twitter : https://twitter.com/IsPharmacology
Facebook: https://www.facebook.com/ispharmacology.difficult.5
Instagram: https://www.instagram.com/ispharmacologydifficult/
Youtube:
https://www.youtube.com/channel/UC-LnUrZKlcBuQaLa2HDQOVg